Designed For Success

Superboats

Revised & Updated

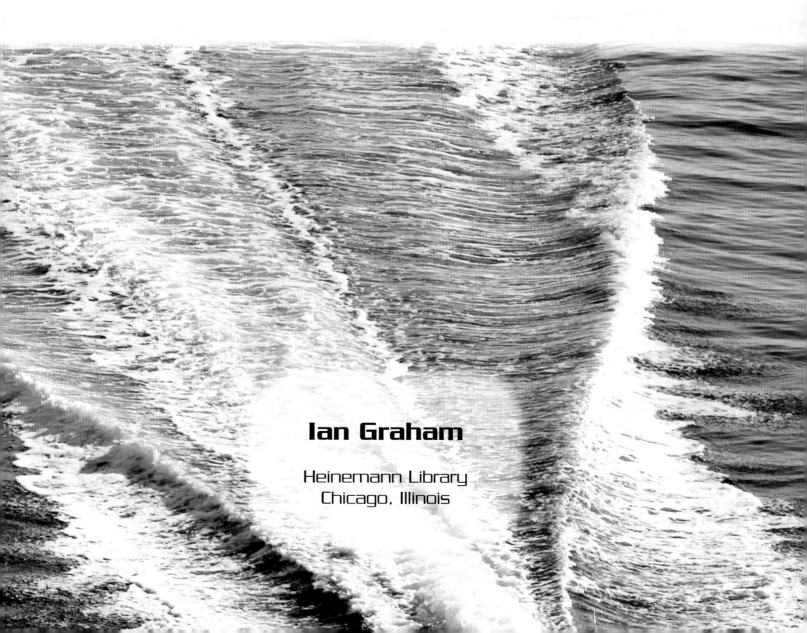

Ian Graham

Heinemann Library
Chicago, Illinois

Editorial: Andrew Farrow, Patrick Catel, and Harriet Milles
Design: Steven Mead and Geoff Ward
Illustrations: Geoff Ward
Picture Research: Melissa Allison
Production: Alison Parsons

Originated by Modern Age
Printed and bound in China by South China Printing Company

13 12 11 10 09 08
10 9 8 7 6 5 4 3 2 1

Library of Congress Cataloging-in-Publication Data
Graham, Ian, 1953 –
   Superboats / Ian Graham.
      p. cm. – (Designed for Success)
Summary: Descibes the specifications, safety equipment, and uses of a
variety of fast, powerful, and luxurious powerboats, including ski-boats,
motor yachts, one-person hydroplanes, and 2000-horsepower offshore
racing powerboats.
Includes bibliographical references and index.
ISBN 978-1-432-91649-7 (Library binding-hardcover)
1. Motorboats—Juvenile literature. [1. Motorboats.] I. Title. II. Series.
      VM341 .G7324 2003
      623.8'231—dc21

Acknowledgments
The publishers would like to thank the following for permission to reproduce photographs: © Alvey & Towers pp. **5** (bottom), **7** (top), **11** (top), **11** (bottom), **25** (bottom); © TIPS/GERARD VANDYSTADT/VANDYSTADT p. **4**; © Australian National Maritime Museum p. **27** (bottom); © Corbis pp. **18**, **19** (top), **19** (bottom); © Kos Picture Source/G-J Norman p. **8**; © Kos Picture Source/Gilles Martin-Raget p. **23** (top); © Miss Freei p. **27** (top); © Nautica International p. **21**; © PA Photos pp. **16** (large picture), **28**; © PA Photos/Ben Curtis p. **26**; © PA Photos/Chris Ison p. **9** (bottom); © PA Photos/EPA pp. **9** (top), **25** (top); © Princess International p. **5** (top); © Powerboatp1.com pp. **10**, **15** (top); © R. D. Battersby/Tografox pp. **11** (middle), **12**, **13** (top), **13** (bottom left), **13** (bottom right), **15** (bottom), **24**; © Richard Page of Gingerpix by courtesy of the RYA p. **21** (bottom); © Rick Tomlinson Photography p. **25** (middle); © Skiers Choice p. **6**; © Steven Piantieri p. **16** (inset); © Sunseeker p. **14**; © TRH Pictures/Sealine p. **23** (bottom); © TRH/Racal Decca p. **7** (bottom); © TRH/US Navy p. **17** (bottom); © US Library of Congress p. **29**; © WireImage.com/CityFiles p. **11** (middle).

Cover photograph reproduced with permission of © TIPS Images/GERARD VANDYSTADT/VANDYSTADT. Background images by © istockphoto/Nicholas Rjabow and © istockphoto.

Our thanks to Mark Wheeler for his help in the preparation of the first edition of this book.

Every effort has been made to contact copyright holders of any material reproduced in this book. Any omissions will be rectified in subsequent printings if notice is given to the publishers.

Disclaimer
All the Internet addresses (URLs) given in this book were valid at the time of going to press. However, due to the dynamic nature of the Internet, some addresses may have changed, or sites may have ceased to exist since publication. While the author and publishers regret any inconvenience this may cause readers, no responsibility for any such changes can be accepted by either the author or the publishers.

▷ Contents

SUPERBOATS

Any words appearing in the text in bold, **like this**, are explained in the glossary.

High-Performance Boats

High-**performance** boats are the fastest, most powerful, and most luxurious of powerboats. They are enjoyed and raced on the world's rivers, lakes, and seas. They range from **personal watercraft** to luxurious motor yachts, and from tiny one-person **hydroplanes** to roaring 2,000-**horsepower**, offshore racing powerboats. They can have one, two, or even three hulls.

The hull is the part of a boat that sits in the water. Many high-performance boats have hulls called **planing hulls**. These are designed to ride on top of the water instead of trying to push their way through it. **Hydrofoil** boats ride on underwater **planes** that lift their hulls above the surface of the water altogether.

Offshore racers ▽

Racing powerboats, like this **catamaran**, can race around an offshore course at average speeds of more than 110 **knots** (125 mph/200 kph). At top speed they carve up the surf and leap from wave to wave. To keep up this sort of performance for a whole race, these racing boats have to be immensely powerful and strong.

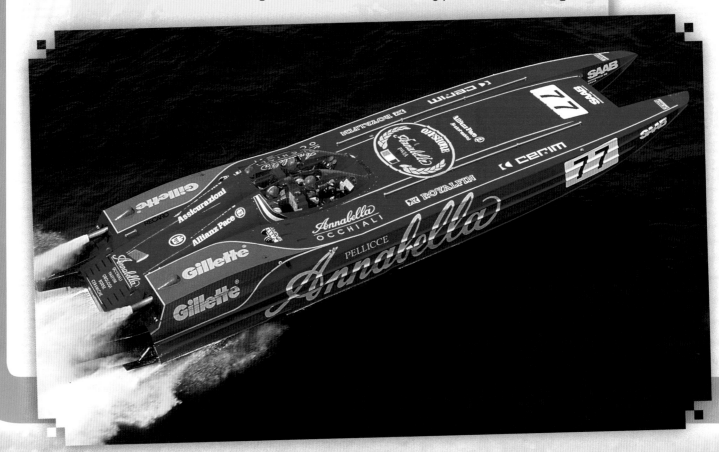

◁ Royalty afloat

The Princess V65 is a modern luxury motor yacht. The 65.6-foot boat is powered by twin high-speed **diesel engines**. These two powerful engines give it a top speed of 38 knots, or about 44 mph (70 kph). Its hull is designed to combine fast and efficient **propulsion** with a stable, comfortable ride. The yacht's luxurious interior includes a home entertainment center with television, DVD, VCR, hi-fi, and surround sound. And it has built-in twin garages for small boats or personal watercraft!

Design factors

All of these boats have to be designed. They have to be the right shape and weight. They have to be big enough, but not too big. Their engines have to be the right size and power. Cost is an important factor in their design. They have to be affordable, and they have to look good, too. A boat's designer has to consider all of these matters.

PRINCESS V65 SPORTS CRUISER

Length: 66.6 feet (20.3 m)

Width: 16.7 feet (5.1 m)

Engine: twin diesels up to 1,360 hp

Propulsion: **propeller**

Top speed: 38 knots (44 mph/70 kph)

Come fly with me! ▷

Passengers can skim over the tops of the waves in hydrofoils. When a hydrofoil takes off, it is not slowed down or buffeted by surface waves anymore. This gives its passengers a much faster and smoother journey. When passenger hydrofoils became popular in the 1950s, they were so much faster than existing boats that they slashed some journey times by three-quarters.

Sport and Pleasure Boats

Sport and pleasure boats are designed for the activity for which they will be used. For example, this might be luxury cruising or it might be towing water-skiers. The form (shape) of the boat depends on what it will be used for.

Sport and pleasure boats are mostly **monohulls**. The single hull has lots of room inside for seating, engines, and, in larger boats, cabins. The bow (front) of the hull is V-shaped to cut through the water. A deep V-hull is more comfortable than a broad, shallow V-hull, because the boat rolls less from side-to-side. However, a broader V-hull has more space inside. The designer has to balance these factors.

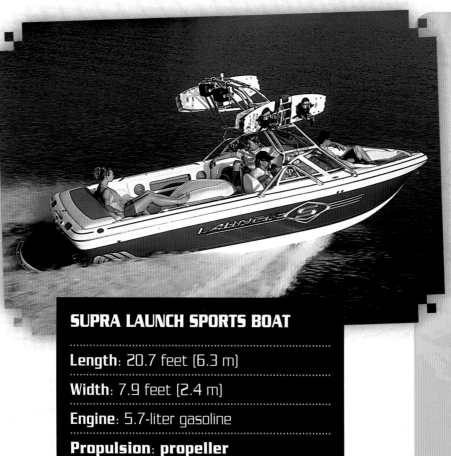

SUPRA LAUNCH SPORTS BOAT

Length: 20.7 feet (6.3 m)

Width: 7.9 feet (2.4 m)

Engine: 5.7-liter gasoline

Propulsion: **propeller**

Top speed: 37 **knots** (42 mph/68 kph)

◁ Wake up!

All boats create a **wake** behind them—a trail of churned-up water. Sport boats are now designed to produce the right shape of wake for different water sports! For example, **wakeboarders** like a higher wake than water-skiers for doing tricks. Some boats are designed to let the driver change the shape of the wake. Pumping water into **ballast** tanks raises or lowers the bow and changes the wake's shape. The Supra Launch uses a different system. It has an adjustable wake board at the stern (rear). Raising or lowering the board changes the shape of the wake.

◁ GPS marks the spot

For centuries, sailors steered by the sun and stars or by measuring how fast they traveled for a certain time in a particular direction. However, these methods were not very accurate. Then the U.S. government developed a Global Positioning System (GPS) so that its military forces could find their precise location. Now everyone can use it. A GPS receiver picks up radio signals from satellites orbiting Earth. It figures out how far away the satellites are and, from this information, calculates its exact position.

Seeing with radio ▽

Most large, seagoing powerboats are equipped with radar. Radar can "see" at night and in fog. It sends out bursts of radio waves in all directions and picks up any reflections that bounce back off objects, such as other boats. The reflections are shown on a screen.

Look out!

A clear view around a boat is vital to avoid accidents. A speedboat driver can sit down in the hull and have a good view because the boat is so small and sits so low in the water. Larger motor yachts need a raised **cockpit** or bridge above their cabins so the driver can see all around the boat.

Racing Powerboats

Racing boats are designed differently from leisure boats. Speed and strength are more important than comfort and space for cabins, sun decks, and baggage storage.

If the boat is to be a **monohull**, a long, narrow, V-shaped **planing hull** works well. The V-shaped bow (front) cuts through the waves easily, and the planing hull is fast over the water. Its long, narrow shape also reduces **air resistance**. The stern (rear) of the boat houses a powerful gasoline or **diesel engine**.

Most big racing boats today are **catamarans**—they have two hulls side-by-side. Catamarans are popular because their two ultra-slim hulls slip through the water faster than one big hull. The wide shape of the boat means that it rolls less from side-to-side than a monohull. Power is supplied by engines in each hull. A high-power "cat" like the *Spirit of Norway* can reach more than 130 **knots** (150 mph/240 kph) when racing at full speed in calm water.

Go-fast boats ▷

The cigarette boat is a long, slender monohull powerboat used in offshore racing. Cigarette boats, which are also known as go-fast boats, are up to about 50 feet long, with a hull shaped like a deep V. Two or more engines power a cigarette boat through the water at up to about 80 knots (95 mph or 150 kph).

Racing in a bubble ▷

So much of a racing powerboat sits above the water that its **performance** in air is as important as its performance in water. To cut down air resistance, the fastest racing boats have enclosed **cockpits**. The crew sits under a **streamlined**, bubble-shaped canopy. Some of the big racing cats have a cockpit in each hull.

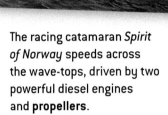

SPIRIT OF NORWAY RACING CAT

Length: 46.6 feet (14.2 m)

Width: 13 feet (4 m)

Engine: 2 x 8.2-liter **V12s**

Propulsion: propeller

Top speed: 130+ knots (150+ mph/240+ kph)

The racing catamaran *Spirit of Norway* speeds across the wave-tops, driven by two powerful diesel engines and **propellers**.

Stepping out ▽

The bottom of a racing hull is not perfectly smooth. It looks as if it has been cut from side-to-side, and the front section sits a little lower than the rear section. It is called a **stepped hull**. As the boat accelerates, it rises up onto the lowest part of the hull. This reduces **drag**, because less of the hull has to push through the water. Air is sucked underneath the hull along channels at each side of the step. The mixture of air and water under the boat reduces drag even more. It works like oil lubricating the moving parts of an engine and lets the boat go much faster.

The stepped hull is clearly visible on boat C-54. It looks as if someone has cut slices into the boat!

Sunseeker Challenger
DESIGN FLAIR

The Sunseeker Challenger is a world-class high-**performance** racing powerboat. Its slim, elegant hull is about 39 feet long and **stepped** underneath. It is designed to skim effortlessly across the water's surface at high speed. Its clean lines are designed to cut **drag** and **air resistance** to a minimum. A shallow windshield in front of the **cockpit** deflects air up and over the crew. The cockpit is also designed for racing, with separate side-by-side seats for a crew of two.

Power for the Challenger is supplied by twin 480-**horsepower diesel engines** driving two "surface-piercing" **propellers**. By using a combination of materials carefully chosen for strength and lightness, the boat's weight has been kept down to 9,920 pounds. Keeping weight down is important, because a lighter boat can accelerate faster and reach higher speeds.

The sleek, slender Sunseeker Challenger is designed to be one of the world's fastest powerboats.

Snorkeling

The Challenger's special propellers are called surface-piercing propellers because they are designed to work best with only their bottom half underwater. However, when the boat sets off, the propellers are completely submerged. To ensure that they work at their best, a pipe supplies the top half of each propeller with air from the surface. The pipes, called snorkels, enable the propellers to spin more freely. They come up to speed faster while the boat accelerates to its **planing** speed.

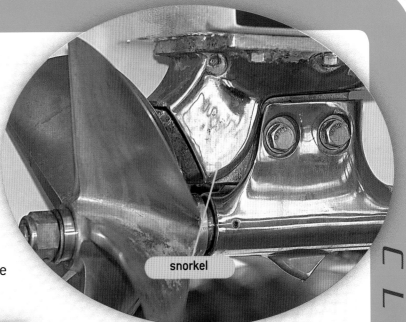

snorkel

Design rules

Racing boats are designed according to a set of rules. There are two classes (types) of Powerboat P1 boat—the Evolution Class and the SuperSport Class. Challenger is a SuperSport boat. These boats must be 32.8 to 42 feet long, with gasoline engines up to 8.3 liters or diesel engines up to 6 liters.

Anti-stuff nose

Ideally, a designer would like a boat to sit absolutely level as it speeds across flat, calm water. Unfortunately, the sea is rarely flat and calm. Therefore the boat is certain to roll and pitch as it hits waves and troughs in the water. In rough water, the Challenger's nose might actually pitch down low enough to plow under the surface. Its nose has two 7-inch wings, called anti-stuff planes, designed to lift the nose and get it out of the water again fast.

anti-stuff plane

CLOSER LOOK

Sunseeker Challenger
LIGHTNESS IN STRENGTH

The Sunseeker Challenger is built from materials called composites, which are chosen for their strength and lightness. The main part of the hull is made from **glass reinforced plastic (GRP)**. It is called a composite because it is made from at least two different materials—in this case, a plastic called **epoxy** and **glass fiber**. The composite made from them is stronger than either of the separate materials.

GRP is an ideal material for making boats because it can be molded into almost any shape. Traditional wooden hulls can rot if they are not painted or varnished to stop water from soaking into them. GRP does not rot or need as much maintenance as wood. The parts of the hull that have to be the strongest are made from Kevlar, a composite material made from plastic fibers instead of glass fibers.

Making glass hulls

Construction of a GRP hull begins with a mold that looks like the boat's hull turned inside out.

- First, the mold is painted with something called a releasing agent so that the hull will not stick to it.
- Next, a thick gel coat is painted onto the mold. This forms the smooth outer surface of the hull.
- Mats of hair-thin strands of glass are laid on top of the gel and soaked with liquid epoxy resin.
- When the resin sets hard, the hull is pulled out of the mold.

Flimsy hull

A GRP hull on its own is almost as flimsy as molded gelatin. Designers add parts to strengthen it so that it holds its shape. The strengthening parts that run the length of the boat are called stringers. Those that run across the hull are called bulkheads. They lock the hull into the correct shape so that it does not buckle when waves hit it. Then the fuel tanks are installed in the hull. The molded deck is placed on top of the hull and bonded (glued) to it. The propellers and driving controls are fitted. Finally, the boat's diesel engines are installed.

A new powerboat is lowered into the water for trials.

Weight taming

A racing boat's engines, like the twin diesel engines shown here, are the heaviest parts of the boat. They have to be positioned in exactly the right place. If they were too far forward, the boat's bow (front) would sit too low. If they were too far back, the bow would sit too high. They also have to be mounted securely so that they cannot move. They are bolted to metal plates molded into the hull.

Sunseeker Challenger
PURE PERFORMANCE

The Sunseeker Challenger is one of the world's fastest powerboats. Challenger and all the other boats that race in the SuperSport Championship must have the same hull and engines as the production boats that anyone can buy. Challenger is based on the record-breaking Sunseeker XS2000 powerboat.

Like the XS2000, Challenger has a **planing hull**. As the boat accelerates, it rises up into the planing position, skimming across the water's surface. At top speed, it can reach nearly 85 **knots** (87 mph/140 kph). It races in the sea, where it can face waves several feet high. The crew members sit in an open cockpit. Challenger competes against about 20 other high-performance boats built according to the same rules. The races are held close to the shore, so that lots of people can see them. There are two types of race—rallies and endurance races. Rallies must be at least 50 nautical miles (55 miles/95 kilometers) long. Endurance races are longer, at least 80 nautical miles (90 miles/150 kilometers).

World-beater

On July 24, 2001, a standard XS2000, like the one on the right, set four world records and two British records.

- It became the fastest boat over 6, 12, 18, and 24 hours.

- In 24 hours circling the Isle of Wight, off the south coast of England, it covered a distance of 1,099 miles (1,770 kilometers) at an average speed of 46 knots (52 mph/85 kph).

- It also set new British records for the fastest five-lap and ten-lap times around the Isle of Wight.

Cockpit crew

The rules for SuperSport boats say that they can have a crew of up to three people. The three are the driver, throttleman, and navigator. The driver steers the boat, while the throttleman controls the engine and the navigator figures out the best course (direction) to steer. The Sunseeker Challenger has a crew of two—a driver/navigator and throttleman.

Down to a turn

Challenger is steered by turning a steering wheel in the cockpit, which turns a **rudder** behind each propeller. A rudder is a panel that can swivel to one side so that it lies at an angle to the water rushing past the boat. The water hits the rudder and pushes the stern (rear) of the boat to one side, swinging the front end round to point in a new direction.

SUNSEEKER CHALLENGER

Length: 38.9 feet (11.85 m)

Width: 7.5 feet (2.3 m)

Engine: twin 420-hp diesels

Propulsion: propellers

Top speed: 74 knots (85 mph/137 kph)

rudder

propeller

CLOSER LOOK

Engine Power

Most boats are powered by the same sort of gasoline and **diesel** piston engines that power cars. The most exotic boats are propelled by jet engines.

A boat's engine may be **outboard** (hung on the outside) or **inboard** (housed inside the hull). This choice affects the design of the hull and the way the boat is steered.

- Boats with outboard engines are steered by turning the whole engine and **propeller**. Bigger engines are housed inside the hull, and the boat is usually steered by turning a **rudder**.

- Some powerboats use a system called a stern-drive, or out-drive. This enables a boat with an inboard engine to steer by swiveling the propeller.

- A few large, fast boats use **water-jet engines**. They pump water out of the boat's stern at high speed.

- A handful of boats use jet engines. The engine can propel the boat by jet **thrust**, like a jet airplane, or by spinning a shaft that drives a propeller or water-jet.

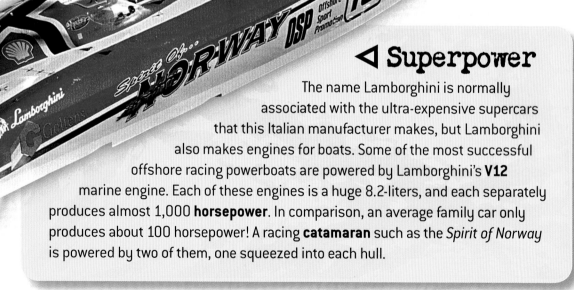

◁ Superpower

The name Lamborghini is normally associated with the ultra-expensive supercars that this Italian manufacturer makes, but Lamborghini also makes engines for boats. Some of the most successful offshore racing powerboats are powered by Lamborghini's **V12** marine engine. Each of these engines is a huge 8.2-liters, and each separately produces almost 1,000 **horsepower**. In comparison, an average family car only produces about 100 horsepower! A racing **catamaran** such as the *Spirit of Norway* is powered by two of them, one squeezed into each hull.

Pushy blades ▷

A propeller works by producing a force that pushes a boat through the water. Its blades are set at an angle so that when the propeller spins, they push backward against the water. Most boat propellers are completely submerged, but high-**performance** boats often use propellers that run with half the propeller blades out of the water at any given time. They are called surface-piercing propellers. They are larger and spin more slowly than submerged propellers. Surprisingly, this makes them more efficient than smaller, faster, submerged propellers.

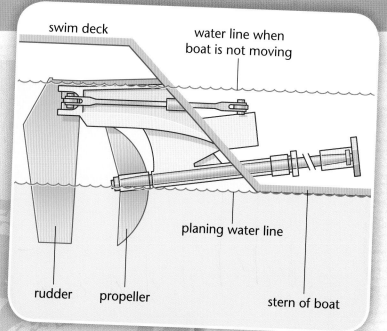

swim deck

water line when boat is not moving

planing water line

rudder   propeller   stern of boat

◁ Fly Navy

A **hydrofoil** is a boat that uses underwater wings to lift its hull out of the water. The U.S. Navy gunboat *Tucumcari* was the first large hydrofoil to be powered by a water-jet engine instead of propellers. It was launched in 1967.

TUCUMCARI

The 72-feet long, 64-ton *Tucumcari* could travel at nearly 50 **knots** (56 mph/90 kph) in all weather.

Hydroplanes

Hydroplanes are the Grand Prix racers of the boating world. These small, light boats skim across the water's surface incredibly fast. Hydroplanes are designed to ride on top of the water, not through it. As a hydroplane speeds up, air rushes into a tunnel under the boat. It is the pressure of this trapped air that pushes the boat upward. Eventually, the boat rises up so high that it touches the water at only three points—two floats, called sponsons, at the front, and the **propeller** at the back. For this reason, these boats are also called three-point hydroplanes, or prop-riders.

Older **inboard** hydroplanes had their engine at the front, with the driver sitting behind. Modern inboard hydroplanes, called cabovers, are designed the opposite way. The engine is at the back and the driver sits at the front. The cabover design is faster because the engine is mounted lower down. This lets the boat turn faster without tipping over.

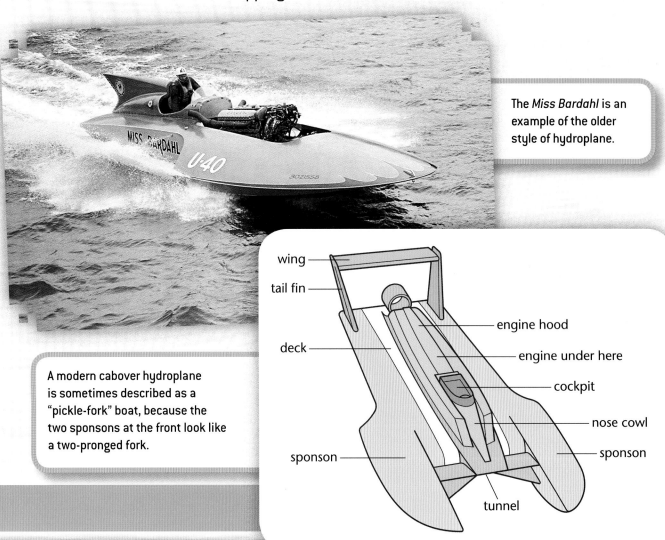

The *Miss Bardahl* is an example of the older style of hydroplane.

A modern cabover hydroplane is sometimes described as a "pickle-fork" boat, because the two sponsons at the front look like a two-pronged fork.

wing

tail fin

deck

engine hood

engine under here

cockpit

nose cowl

sponson

sponson

tunnel

SUPERBOATS

Wave dancer △

When the U-25 hydroplane (called *Miss Freei*) dances across the water, it barely touches the surface. The opening above the **cockpit** sucks air into a **gas turbine engine** that came from a Chinook military helicopter. *Miss Freei* held the world speed record for a propeller driver boat until 2004, with an average speed of 179 **knots** (205 mph/330 kph).

MISS FREEI HYDROPLANE

Length: 29.9 feet (9.1 m)

Width: 14.4 feet (4.4 m)

Engine: Lycoming L7C gas turbine

Propulsion: propeller

Top speed: 191 knots (220 mph/355 kph)

Skid turns ▷

When a car or bicycle turns, it pushes against the ground in one direction to turn in the opposite direction. A hydroplane skimming over the water also needs something to push against, or it cannot turn. A small fin, called a skid fin, dips under the water's surface. As the boat turns, the skid fin pushes against the water and stops the boat from sliding sideways.

skid fin

Floating on Air

Rescue services and security forces use boats called RIBs (Rigid **Inflatable** Boats) because they are small, fast, and light. RIBs range from tiny rowing boat-sized models for use on lakes and rivers to bigger offshore and oceangoing boats. The same design features make them very good for leisure, sports, and racing.

RIBs have a rigid hull with an inflated tube, or collar, around the top to give them **buoyancy**. Being inflatable, they are extremely light, easy to handle, and virtually unsinkable.

- The air-filled collar is divided into a series of watertight compartments. If one is pierced, the others stay inflated and keep the boat afloat.
- The RIB's hull is V-shaped at the bow (front) and flatter at the stern (rear), forming a **planing** surface that rides on top of the water.
- The hull is usually made from **glass reinforced plastic (GRP)**.
- The collar is made from a sandwich of materials that are tough, flexible, and airtight.

Rubber sandwiches ▽

RIB collars are made from a sandwich of at least three different materials. A tough tube of polyester fabric is lined with a rubberlike material, such as neoprene. The polyester gives the tube strength so that it does not tear apart. The lining material makes it airtight. On the outside, the polyester is covered with a layer of tough plastic material. This covering provides a smooth outer surface and protects the collar from oil, gasoline, and ultraviolet rays in sunlight.

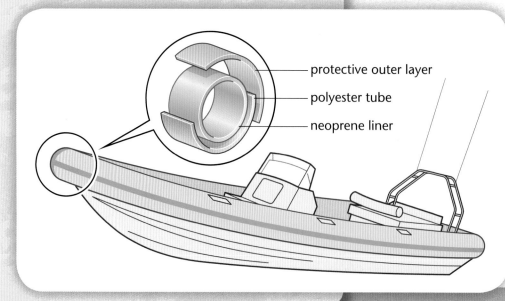

protective outer layer
polyester tube
neoprene liner

Cat RIBs ▷

Most RIBs are **monohulls**, but they can be made in any shape. **Catamaran** RIBs are very popular because of the extra stability their twin-hull design gives them. The Nautica RIB 20 is a catamaran RIB with a ramp in the bow. It can use the ramp as a diving platform at sea, or lower it on a beach to unload people or cargo.

Super RIB ▽

RIBs have become so popular that there are now luxury models and racing versions. *Hot Lemon V* (shown here) is a high-**performance** RIB. It is the latest in a series of record-breaking Hot Lemons. In 2005 *Hot Lemon V* set a new record for sailing around Great Britain. Mike and Dave Deacon sailed it around Britain in 31 hours 22 minutes and 46 seconds. Two earlier boats, *Hot Lemon III* and *Hot Lemon IV*, set Round Britain records in 2001 and 2002, respectively.

HOT LEMON V

Length: 32.8 feet (10.0 m)

Width: 9.8 feet (3.0 m)

Engine: 315-**hp diesels**

Propulsion: **propellers**

Top speed: 65 **knots** (75 mph/120 kph)

SUPERBOATS

21

Hydrofoils are designed to go faster than other boats by "flying" above the water. They use underwater wings to lift their hull out of the water altogether.

When a hydrofoil sits at rest, it looks much the same as any other boat. As it sets off and speeds up, something strange happens. The hull rises up, and eventually the boat takes off and flies above the water. Its weight is supported by wings, called **foils**, that are designed to "fly" through water. They are tiny compared to aircraft wings, because water is thicker than air. A small foil slowly cutting through water can produce as much **lift** as a big wing slicing much faster through the air. Lifting the hull out of the water cuts the **drag** it normally produces and lets the boat travel faster while also burning less fuel. Underwater foils are not affected by waves on the surface, so hydrofoils can sail smoothly in bad weather.

"V" for hydrofoil ▽

Most passenger hydrofoils are fitted with V-shaped foils. They automatically keep the boat at the right height. If the boat loses height as it flies along, more of the V-foils sink under the water. There, they produce more lift, and so the boat rises again. If it rises too high, more of the V-foils come up out of the water. They produce less lift, and the boat settles down lower again.

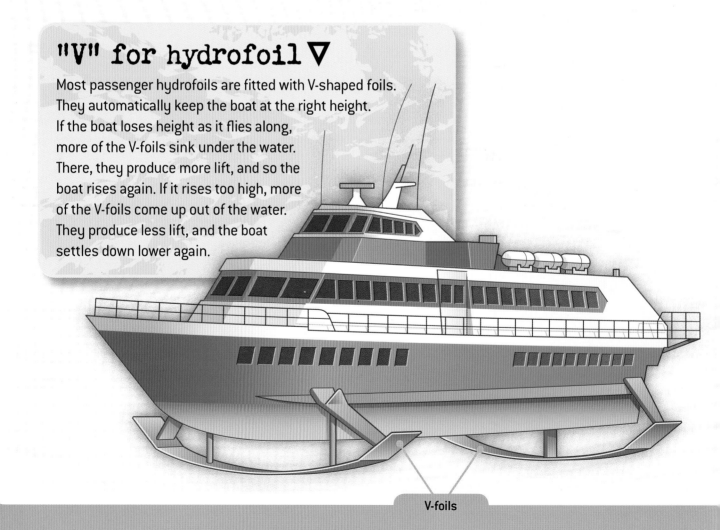

V-foils

◁ Flying sailboats

Sailboats can fly, too. *Hydroptère* is a hydrofoil sailboat. It has three foils— one at each side of its hull and a third in the shape of an upside-down "T" at its stern. The T-foil also acts as a **rudder**. The 69-foot long, 10,800-pound boat reached a top speed of 41 **knots** (47 mph/76 kph) in sea trials.

Jet boats ▽

The Boeing Jetfoil is a **water-jet**-powered hydrofoil. As it flies along, it measures its height above the water by bouncing **ultrasonic** sound waves off the water and timing how long they take to come back. Information from this and other instruments controls the position of the flaps in its underwater foils. Swiveling the flaps controls the boat's height.

BOEING 929-100 JETFOIL

Length: 89.9 feet (27.4 m)

Width: 29.9 feet (9.1 m)

Engine: 2 x jet engines

Propulsion: water-jets

Top speed: 46 knots (53 mph/85 kph)

Safety First

Designers and boat-builders make their boats as safe as possible, but accidents can still happen. So, boats of all sizes carry extra safety equipment designed to protect the crew and passengers.

Safety equipment used on water is designed to work in two different ways. First, it ensures that people stay afloat and then, if necessary, it calls for help. If any crew or passengers fall in the water, life jackets and, on larger boats, life rafts keep them afloat. If help is needed, radio, lights, and flares attract attention. Safety is particularly important in racing, where things can go spectacularly wrong in the blink of an eye. Racing boat crews are often cocooned inside a "survival cell" similar to the **cockpit** of a Formula 1 race car—and they wear similar safety clothing, too.

Staying afloat ▽

The most important piece of safety equipment carried at sea is the life jacket. There are two types. Both are designed to keep someone afloat if he or she falls into water.

- The first type is filled with foam plastic. Air bubbles in the foam make them very **buoyant**. However, the foam also makes them quite bulky and cumbersome.
- The second type (pictured below) is lighter and thinner. When it is needed, it is filled up with gas from a small, built-in cylinder. These **inflatable** jackets are either operated by the wearer or they may be triggered automatically when they hit water.

A high-**performance** boat can turn over in a fraction of a second if it hits a wave or another boat's **wake** at an awkward angle.

This picture shows a flare being used by a man overboard.

Flaring up ▷

If a boat has no radio, or the radio is not working, the crew members need another way of signaling that they need help. They can get help and show where they are by using flares. A flare is designed to burn slowly, like a large match, and produce lots of light or smoke, or both. Parachute flares are fired up into the sky and descend slowly under a mini-parachute.

◁ Staying alive

Racing boat crews wear a life jacket and a crash helmet. An intercom built into each helmet lets the crew members talk to each other. Crew members thrown overboard may be unconscious, so their life jackets are designed to turn them over on to their backs to keep their faces out of the water.

Record Setters

The boats that set speed records are extremely high-**performance** boats. They combine the most powerful engines with the sleekest hulls to reach the highest speeds.

The designers of high-performance boats sometimes use parts designed for other fast vehicles. Jet engines developed for use in helicopters and fighters are often put to use in boats specially designed to break records. Helicopter engines are designed to spin a rotor, so they can be easily modified to spin a boat's **propeller** instead. Fighter engines are designed to propel a plane by jet **thrust**, and they are used in the same way in record-breaking boats. The boat is pushed along by the jet of fiery hot gas produced by the engine. The shape of the boat is very important, too. Record-breakers often use the shape that is most successful in racing—the **hydroplane**.

Around-the-world adventure▽

In 1998 the dramatic design of the powerboat *Cable & Wireless Adventurer* enabled it to sail around the world faster than any other boat had done before. It was designed as a type of **monohull** called a very slender vessel (VSV). A VSV is very fast, but its long, slim hull rolls a lot in heavy seas. To stop this, *Adventurer* has two smaller **outrigger** floats attached to the main hull. The 115-foot, 55-ton boat circled the globe in 75 days—8 days faster than the previous record-holder, the U.S. nuclear submarine *Triton*.

Prop record

On March 13, 2004, a hydroplane called *Miss Budweiser* made history. With Dave Villwock at the controls, it skimmed across the surface of Lake Oroville in California at a speed of 220 mph (354 kph). It was the highest speed that any propeller-driven boat had reached. The boat had to make two mile-long runs within 20 minutes, and then its average speed was calculated.

Star performer ▽

On October 8, 1978, Ken Warby became the fastest person ever to travel on water. He set a record speed of 276 **knots** (317 mph/511 kph) in his boat *Spirit of Australia* on Blowering Dam Lake in Australia. Warby built the boat himself. He chose a Westinghouse J34 jet engine to provide the enormous thrust he needed.

MISS BUDWEISER HYDROPLANE

Length: 29.5 feet (9.0 m)

Width: 14.4 feet (4.4 m)

Engine: **gas turbine**

Propulsion: propeller

Top speed: 197 knots (227 mph/365 kph)

▷ Data Files

Leisure and racing powerboats vary a great deal in their size, means of **propulsion**, and **performance**. Here is data for a range of these boats.

Boat	Length (feet)	Width (feet)	Propulsion	Top speed (knots / mph)
Boeing 929-100 Jetfoil	89.9	29.9	**Water-jet**	46 / 53
Cable & Wireless Adventurer	114.8	46.3	**Propeller**	27 / 31
Top Gun cigarette powerboat	37.4	7.9	Propeller	78 / 90
Hot Lemon V RIB	32.8	9.8	Propeller	65 / 75
Hydroptère hydrofoil yacht	68.9	60	Sail	41 / 47
Miss Freei hydroplane	29.9	14.4	Propeller	179 / 220
Princess V65 sports cruiser	66.6	16.7	Propeller	38 / 44
Spirit of Australia hydroplane	26.9	7.9	Jet Thrust	276 / 317
Spirit of Norway racing **catamaran**	46.6	13	Propeller	130+ / 150+
Sunseeker Challenger	38.9	7.5	Propeller	74 / 85
Supra Launch sports boat	20.7	7.9	Propeller	37 / 42

Jet boat ▷

The first boat powered by jet **thrust** to set an outright world water speed record was the *Bluebird K7* **hydroplane** driven by Donald Campbell. Between 1955 and 1964, Campbell set seven world water speed records in the boat and raised the record from 155 **knots** (178 mph/287 kph) to 241 knots (276 mph/445 kph). In 1964 he also held the land speed record, making him the only person ever to hold both the land and water speed records at the same time.

S U P E R B O A T S

Further Information ◁

Books

Bullard, Lisa. *Powerboats*. Minneapolis: Lerner, 2004.

Dubowski, Mark. *Superfast Boats*. New York: Bearport, 2005.

Sautter, Aaron. *Speedboats*. Mankato, Minn.: Capstone, 2007.

Savage, Jeff. *Hydroplane Boats*. Mankato, Minn.: Capstone, 2004.

Websites

www.boatsafe.com/kids

An excellent website that answers lots of questions about boats

http://boatingsidekicks.com/kidsknow/knowmain.htm

A website full of lots of boating know-how from the National Safe Boating Council

http://pbskids.org/zoom/activities/sci/sodabottleboat.html

Make your own speedboat from a soda bottle

First foiler ▷

The first **hydrofoil** boat (pictured right) was built in 1905 by its inventor, Enrico Forlanini. The **foils** were stacked up above each other like the rungs of a ladder. Alexander Graham Bell, the inventor of the telephone, bought a licence from Forlanini to build his hydrofoils in the United States.

Glossary

air resistance force of air pushing against anything that tries to move through it

ballast heavy substance placed in the bottom of a boat to make it more stable. Water can be used as ballast.

buoyant/buoyancy ability to float. If something is buoyant, it floats.

catamaran type of boat with two hulls side-by-side instead of one. Catamarans are sometimes called "cats."

cockpit part of a sport or racing boat where the crew sits

diesel engine type of engine used by larger boats because of its power and reliability

drag force that slows a boat down as it moves through water

epoxy resin liquid chemical that sets hard, which is used in boat-building

foil short for "hydrofoil," a wing-shaped part of a hydrofoil boat. Underwater foils cut through the water and create a force that lifts the boat's hull out of the water.

gas turbine engine another name for a jet engine

glass fiber material made from mats of hair-thin strands of glass

glass reinforced plastic (GRP) type of material, called a composite, made from glass fibers embedded in plastic

horsepower (hp) unit of measurement of the power of an engine equal to the work done by one horse, or 746 watts of electrical power

hydrofoil type of boat that rises up out of the water on underwater foils as it speeds up

hydroplane type of racing boat designed to skim across the water's surface. Only its two floats (called sponsons) and its propeller dip into the water. Keeping the main part of its hull out of the water reduces drag and makes the boat faster.

inboard inside a boat's hull. An inboard engine sits inside a boat's hull.

inflatable capable of being filled with air. An inflatable boat is made from rubber or plastic filled with air.

knot unit of measurement that is the same as a nautical mile per hour. (1 nautical mile equals 1.15 land miles or 1.85 kilometers.)

lift force that acts upward. A hydrofoil boat's underwater foils create lift as they cut through the water.

monohull type of boat with one hull

outboard outside a boat's hull. An outboard engine is attached to the outside of a boat's hull.

outrigger frame or structure that holds a float out to one side of a boat

performance vehicle's speed, acceleration, stability, and so on

personal watercraft small motorbike-like vehicle designed for having fun close to shore

plane flat surface. The rear part of a power boat's hull is flatter than the bow and designed to skim over the water's surface. This is described as planing.

planing hull type of hull that is designed to rise up on the top of the water when the boat is traveling fast. Planing hulls are usually flattened underneath so that they can skim the water's surface. Planing reduces drag and lets the boat go faster.

propeller part of a boat that spins and pushes the boat through the water

propulsion pushing, or propelling, a boat through water

rudder part of a boat that is swiveled underwater to steer the boat. Water hitting the angled rudder pushes the stern (back end) of the boat to one side and swings its bow (front end) around to point in a new direction.

stepped (hull) type of planing hull divided into two or more sections with a step between them. Stepped hulls reduce drag and let a boat go faster.

streamlined designed to move through air or water easily, producing very little air resistance or drag. Smooth, gently curving shapes are more streamlined than rough or boxy shapes.

thrust force that pushes a boat through the water. Thrust can be produced by a boat's propeller, a jet of water, or a jet of gas from a gas turbine (jet) engine.

ultrasonic waves like sound waves but so high that they cannot be heard by humans

V12 type of engine with 12 cylinders, in two rows of six, set at an angle to each other, forming a V-shape

wake waves that spread out behind a boat as it moves through water. The wake is caused by the boat's hull and propeller(s) churning up the water.

wakeboarder person who skims across the water behind a boat, while standing on a board like a very short surfboard

water-jet engine type of engine that propels a boat by pumping a high-speed jet of water out of the back of the boat. The pump is often driven by a jet engine.

Index

SUPERBOATS